NANO MUSHROOM IDENTIFIER

Rouf Hamza Boda

GenNext Publication

ISBN : 978-93-8022-258-5

Price : ₹ 360

First Published, 2014

Published by

genNext Publication
23, Main Ansari Road, Darya Ganj
New Delhi-110002
Ph. : 23242060, 23261060
Fax : 011-23285914
E-mail: gennext@hotmail.com
Website : www.gyanbooks.com

Laser Typesetting : Gyan Prints (AB-I), Delhi
Printed at : Isha Print.

Cataloging in Publication Data—DK
Courtesy: D.K. Agencies (P) Ltd. <docinfo@dkagencies.com>

Boda, Rouf Hamza.
Nano mushroom identifier / Rouf Hamza Boda.
p. cm.
ISBN 9789380222585

1. Mushrooms—Identification. 2. Photography of plants. I. Title.

DDC 579.6 23

Foreword

Mushrooms have always been treated as something strange. Myths were associated with the mushrooms since the ancient times. Still myths are glued to mushrooms in the villages due to lack of proper awareness. Though Kashmir valley is gold mine of mushroom biodiversity but people exploit only about ten mushrooms out of hundreds of wild mushrooms found in the valley. Mushroom phobia is predominant in the valley. Present book is a beginner's field guide to mushrooms, as well as basic mushroom identifier. It is a basic book for those who want to plunge in to the mushroom world. This book provides general guidelines about mushrooms from collection to identification up to genus level. Book has been written in simple language so that mushroom can be identified from the field itself. Besides this book contains fundamental information about the mushroom photography. Both macroscopic and microscopic characters have been stressed in the book. At the end of the book a short cut key has been provided. This book will be helpful to farmers, students and research scholars.

Rouf Hamza Boda

Preface

During the course of my research I felt need to compile a basic guide for mushroom collection and identification which will unravel the mysteries of the Mushrooms. After few years I began to summarise the fundamental aspects of the mushroom world which culminated in the form of "Nano Mushroom Identifier" a bottom up approach to the mushroom world. This book provides precise first hand information about the mushrooms. I put on record a deep sense of gratitude to Prof. A.H. Wani who guided me to the mushroom world. I also express my sincere gratitude and indebtedness to Prof. N.A. Munsi. I am highly thankful to Akhter Hussian Malik and Dr. Bilal Ahmad wani who accompanied me during my expedition to discover mushroom world. I am obliged to authors and publishers of various books and journals that were consulted during the course of writing this book.

I will welcome suggestions for the improvement of the book and the suggestions will be incorporated in the next enlarged and colourful edition of this book.

Rouf Hamza Boda

Introduction

What we call a "mushroom" is fruiting-body of a fungus, the reproductive part of the fungus that grows above ground and releases spores, the seed like elements from which new fungi are made. Much as fruit is the reproductive organ of a fruit tree, a mushroom is the reproductive organ of a fungus. Typically, spores sprout from the gills, the thin brown tissue found on the underside of the mushroom cap. Borne by the wind, some kinds of spores are capable of travelling great distances from the fruit-body to start their own fungus colonies. Fungi range from simple forms like thread fungi to complex forms like mushrooms. In Greek, the term mushroom was derived from the word sphongs or sphaggos which means sponge or referred to the sponge like structures of the mushroom. Presently mushroom is regarded as a macrofungus with a distinctive fruiting body which can be either epigeous or hypogeous and large enough to be seen with the naked eyes and to be picked by hand. They belong to fungal groups Basidiomycetes and Ascomycetes. Only fruiting body of the mushroom can be seen whereas the rest of the mushroom remains underground as mycelium. Unlike plants, fungi do not manufacture their own food but must absorb their food from an external source. They obtain their food in three ways as: saprophytes that live on dead organic material, symbionts that form mutually beneficial relationships with living organisms, parasites or pathogens that infect living organisms (host). Many forest mushrooms form symbiotic relationships known as mycorrhizae with tree roots. Mycorrhizal mushrooms are critical to the health of their hosts. Mushrooms are important constituents of minor forest produce (secondary produce), they grow on the most abundant biomolecule of this biosphere known as cellulose. Mushrooms can be roughly divided into four categories, those which are fleshy and edible fall into edible mushrooms, mushrooms which are considered to have some medicinal applications are considered to be medicinal mushrooms. Those which are proved to be or suspected to be poisonous are named as poisonous mushrooms. A miscellaneous category which includes a large number of mushrooms whose properties remains less well-defined are tentatively grouped as other mushrooms. Mushrooms offer tremendous applications as they can be used as food and medicines besides playing key ecological roles. They represent as one of the world's greatest untapped resources of nutrition and palatable food of the future. As food, the nutritional value of mushrooms lies between meat and vegetables thus called as mycomeat or vegetable meat. Mushrooms are good sources of energy. They are low in starch and lipids but rich in proteins. The relationship between diet and disease was summarized by father of medicine Hippocrates in the famous words " Let food be your medicine and medicine be your food" this saying suits mushrooms as they are having tremendous medicinal value, which forms basis of medical mycology. Functional food is any modified food ingredient that may provide a heath benefit beyond the traditional nutrients it contains, thus food as well as medicine underpins, the paradigm of functional foods. Ecologically, role of mushrooms is manifested in three forms viz., as parasites as saprophytic mushrooms and finally those which are in symbiosis with their host plants are called myccorhizal mushrooms. The agriculture waste can be converted into food, feed, fuel and fertilizer through cultivation of mushrooms. Fungi are the most diverse organisms after insects on this biosphere. Fungal kingdom has been estimated to be six times larger than the plant kingdom. Of the estimated 1500000 species of fungi, approximately 70,000 have been identified (Hawksworth et. al., 1991) and about 10,000 of them are mushrooms. India also abounds in mushroom diversity due to diverse habitats; of the 2000 species of edible mushrooms reported to be available in the world, 283 are reported from India.

Many economically important mushrooms can be cultivated in the Kashmir valley due to suitable climatic conditions and presence of basic raw materials. Berkely (1876) was the first person to report macro-fungi from the Kashmir. Although, the area provides diverse niches for mushrooms but people know and eat only few mushrooms and the word mushroom has remained confined only to such mushrooms. Regarding mushrooms, different people have carved out different pictures, even in a single village there are different confusing names and views about a single mushroom thus some using the same mushroom for food while others fearing it to be poisonous. Mushroom cultivation is the best possible use of land if one takes into account yield per unit area. There is a wide taxonomic gap which has created myth about mushrooms. This can be removed by proper identification of the mushrooms, their biochemical analysis and cultivation possibilities. This will help to solve demarcation of mushrooms into different groups like poisonous and non-poisonous, cultivable and non-cultivable mushrooms. Mushrooms use vertical space in a mushroom house thus save land. The mushroom mycota of Kashmir stands out as virtually untapped resource for novel foods, medicines and antimicrobials. Thus our present attempt is to help people to identify common mushrooms and use them as food or medicine. This book will also remove superstitious nature of people which haunts the mind of people about the mushrooms since ages viz., people conceive mushrooms as dirty article growing from stools, urine and rotten wood. Present attempt in the form of book can help common people to identify mushrooms easily. Another aim of the book is to imbibe idea of mushroom research in young.

General Shape of a Mushroom

A typical mushroom consists of a cap like structure called pileus and stalk (stem) like structure called stipe, thus looks umbrella like. Mushroom can be described and identified by studying its macroscopic and microscopic features.

Macroscopic Parts

Pileus (cap)- is the prominent horizontal component of a mushroom bearing lamellae/gills or tubes on the underside. It can have a variety of shapes, sizes and colours.

Hymenium- is the spore-bearing layer (containing asci or basidia) in a fruiting body of a fungus. This can be in the form of lamellae or tubes. The attachment of the hymenium to the pileus and stipe can vary in different species. Lamellae/gill spacing can also vary.

Lamellae/gills- are plate like structures on the underside of the pileus. They are arranged radially from the stipe towards the margin of the pileus. Spore-bearing basidia is found on the lamellae.

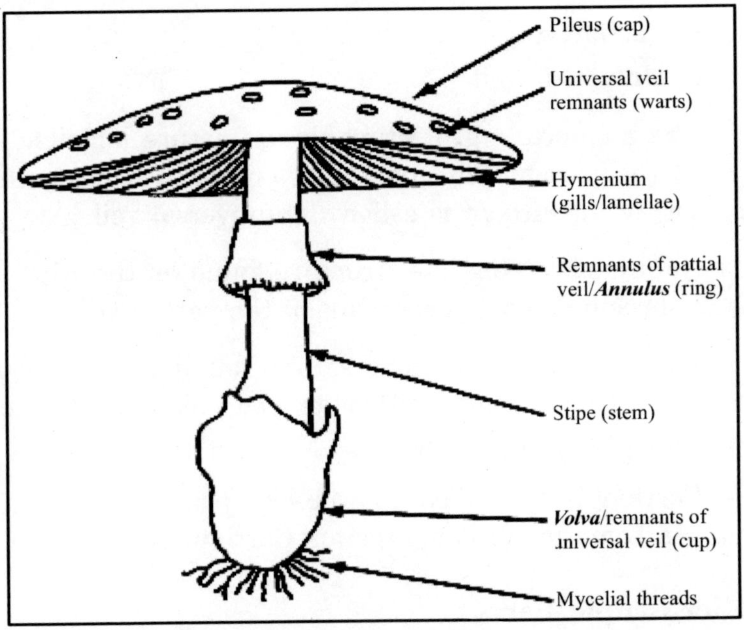

Tubes- instead of gills some mushrooms (genus Boletus) have a thick, sponge-like tube layer with pores of these tubes open to the under surface of the pileus.

Stipe/stalk- is present in most mushrooms and can be attached to the centre, off-centre or to the side of a pileus. Occasionally the stalk can be absent or very small. Stalk-(Stipe) length (from apex to base) as well as the width (both at the apex and and at the base) are used in identification. Other features include the stalk's shape, its surface texture, its colour, and the texture and colour of the context (the flesh or internal tissue). If a ring (annulus) and basal cup (volva) are present, they are described.

Veils- Some mushrooms have membranes referred to as veils that cover and protect the immature mushroom or the immature lamellae. There are two types of veils:

1. Partial veil
2. Universal veil

The membrane protecting the immature lamellae is called the partial veil and the membrane covering the immature mushroom is called the universal veil.

Annulus is a ring like structure found on the stipe of a mushroom. This is a remnant of the partial veil.

Volva is part of the universal veil found at the base of some mushroom stipes, either as a cup like structure or as scaly remnants.

Cortina is the silky, cobweb-like partial veil found only in some mushrooms (genus Cortinarius).

Microscopic Parts

Hyphae is one of the threadlike strands that form the mycelium of the fungus. It consists of a single or double nuclei cells. The wall like structure dividing each cell is known as the septum. A loop like structure called a clamp connection is found at the septum in some fungal hyphae. Mycelium is the mass of hyphae that forms the vegetative part of a fungus.

Ascus - Fungi of class Ascomycetes(e.g Morels) produce spores in a tube-shaped container known as an ascus. Usually an ascus contains 8 spores, which are dispersed through an opening at the tip of the ascus.

Basidia - Fungi of the class Basidiomycetes (e.g Agaricus) produce spores on short appendages called sterigmata that project out of a club shaped basidia. Usually basidia contain 4 spores but sometimes can contain only 2 spores.

Spore - is the reproductive structure of the fungus, which is walled, single or multicelled and is capable of giving rise to a new individual.

Spores-Prints: Spore prints are spore deposits of mushrooms on a paper or on glass slide.

Other-Features

Clamp connections: These are connecting cells between two adjoining hyphal cells, occur only in fungi belonging to the Basidiomycetes. The presence or absence of clamp connections can assist in identifying mushrooms in this group. The length of the basidia or asci and the number of spores produced by them also help to identify some mushrooms. Hymenial cystidia are sterile cells interspersed among the basidia in the hymenium, and their presence or absence can also be important. When they are present, their shape and size are very helpful in indentifying mushrooms.

MUSHROOM IDENTIFICATION

Mushroom identification involves a number of steps viz.

- Mushroom collection from the wild.
- Mushroom photography.

- Study of mushroom habitat.
- Study of mushrooms characters.

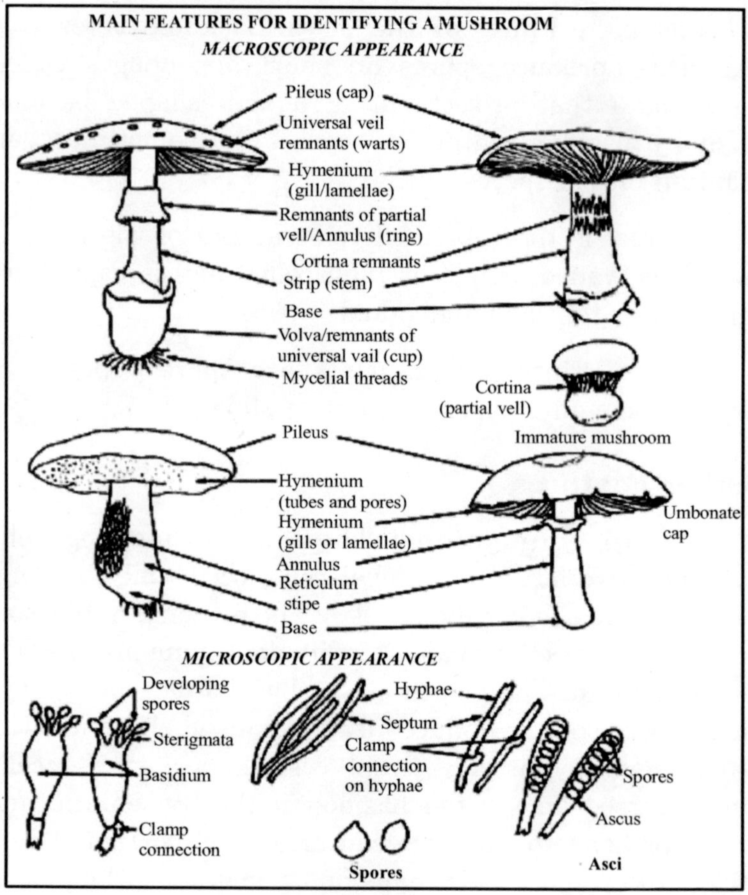

- Listing of mushroom characters.
- Comparing of listed characters with keys to assign them to a particular genus and species.

Mushroom Collection

Arrange mushroom trips in different seasons of the year since different mushrooms grow in different seasons.

Mushroom collection requires some simple equipments viz :

- Willow Baskets for carrying mushrooms.
- Paper bags for wrapping mushroom, note book, pen for noting or drawing key morphological features.
- Knife for digging out mushroom, Fork for finding hypogeous fungi.
- Digital Camera (5 M.P or greater). A tripod stands for holding camera to avoid shaking during Macro mode.
- A stick for searching mushrooms in grass and bushes.
- Also carry a small scale and a digital calliper for measuring the dimensions of a fresh intact mushroom.
- Use colour chart to match the colour of mushroom,
- Storage containers with lids, wax paper roll, small and large paper bags to keep collections from the same location,
- Do carry maps, collecting permits in collection area.
- Use a binocular to see the habitat, whistle for the association of group members.
- Now days solar backpacks are available which can charge your instruments while u are walking through an area.
- A multipurpose small tool which can act as spade as well as adze is good for digging mushrooms.
- A multipurpose tool with small axe and saw for collecting Lignicolous along with the twig.

- One can use flint to make fire if one is camping for nights.
- A vehicle containing tent, and sleeping bag if you are away from the habitation.

Besides this water and some light refreshment is also needed. If you are climbing up a steep area do carry a good griping shoe, lose waterproof clothes (as most mushrooms grow in the rainy season) and a rope. Besides this carry a plastic sheet for bending on knees to photograph mushrooms. Also a good back pack to carry the above mentioned things. Besides using G.P.S and compass one can mark vegetation to retract ones way in jungle. First aid kit should also accompany you.

Mushroom habitat: First thing to look at is to see where a mushroom grows. Knowing the habitat can aid in identification. Some mushrooms are very specific in their host. Mushrooms grow on diverse habitats. Some of the important mushroom habitats are as follows

On the ground in woodlands or associated with trees: Most of the mushrooms in such habitats are mycorrhizal. This relation is symbiotic and benefits both mushroom and host tree. Best example is Bolete, Russula and Lactarius.

On the ground in grassland or open spaces: Such species are generally non mycorrhizal.

Growing on trees, stems or woody debris: Tree growing species may be either dead or living; such species generally secrete extracellular enzymes to degrade cellulose and lignin. Parasitic mushrooms are host specific and perennial. Shelf fungi like polypores generally grow on wood.

Growing in wet situations such as bogs and marshy lands: Mushrooms like Hypholoma and Galerina grow along with mosses.

Growing on burnt ground or on burnt wood: It offers a mineral rich habitat and occurs on newly burnt sites.

Growing on dung or enriched soil: Dung offers moisture and nutrient rich medium, some mushrooms grow on dung of a particular animal only.

Growing on the other fungi: Some mushrooms like mycotrophs grow on other fungi.

Never collect all the specimens of a particular species. Also try to collect only few mushrooms per day because you have to identify them, you cannot identify a number of different specimens overnight. Do not put all the different specimens intermingled in the same basket as it causes mixing of spores of different species and thereby misidentification.

Mushroom Photography

Mushroom photography is an art as well as very essential for identification. A good photograph speaks a lot about mushroom and is half the work in mushroom identification. General guidelines for mushroom photography are as under: get a couple of extra rechargeable batteries and a car charger so you can have extra charged batteries. Now days solar chargers are also available so that you can charge your instruments while on your way. Whenever possible, include a range of specimens (e.g.: buttons to largest caps). Excavate at least one mature specimen, where practicable, to show entire stipe or base. Also catch an entire button, with base toward camera, to show veil remnants, entire base and it colouring, shape, and mycelium, etc. Take a couple of pictures of the top of the mushroom or mushrooms. Take a few pictures of the sides of the mushrooms. Take a couple of pictures of the bottom of the mushroom that shows the stalk. Take pictures of the gills or pores or bottom of the cap of the mushroom. Shoot pictures of the mushroom after it has been cut in half lengthwise to show the inside of the mushroom.

Watch for mycelium, sclerotium, etc. Cut one fruit body in half lengthwise to show features such as gill attachment, colour changes, type of context, etc. Keep an eye on colour changes and show both immediate and delayed reactions. Catch in the photo the local vegetation because some mushrooms are vegetation specific. Also include into the photograph nearby, habitat (needles, cones, dung, rotten wood, soil etc.). Use a reflector or flash to fill in any dense shadows, whether these shadows are produced by sunlight or by the primary flash. This is especially important when the subject has considerable innate contrast, such as a dark cap and a white stipe. Also take different photographs in different modes. Also take photographs of spore prints because they are an aid to mushroom identification. Always take high-Resolution quality pictures in the highest quality and largest picture format you can. This will ensure you have the best quality picture possible. Use a tripod if available, or use something to help steady the camera so you don't get a blurring of the picture. Take several pictures from different angles, with and without a flash. You can always delete pictures you don't like later on. Do carry white and black pieces of plastic sheets to take pictures of the mushrooms if you have to bend on your knees, this will help to give a good colour contrast when taking the pictures. i.e.: dark coloured mushrooms on a light background or light coloured mushrooms on a dark background. In my opinion an SLR camera is the best for photographing mushrooms growing high on the trees.

Mushroom Photography Tips

Try to focus on the following features of different mushroom groups:

- Habit and habitat: Growth Habit (Caespitose, solitary, etc.) Size of overall mushroom. In order to compare the overall size one can include something (a coin etc) that indicates the size of your specimens. Habitat – Is mushroom growing on Wood, Moss, Grass, Twigs, etc.
- Cap surface - Colour or colourless - Scales or scaleless, warts, viscidity, marginal.
- Flesh - Colour and changes on bruising.
- Gill Colour - Cut unopened button in order to observe gill Spacing, width, attachment gill edges
- Annulus - Texture and appearance of unopened specimen
- Staining reaction, if any - All parts
- Fully developed sporocarp showing stature
- Annulus location and characteristics
- Ornamentation on stipe if any
- Stipe base - Bulbous; Taper, etc.
- Tubes - Colour and changes on bruising.
- Pores - Colour, young and old; change(s) on bruising; shape and size; covering when young

- Spore Print - Colour
- Stipe - Size and shape; scabrous? netted? with sticky granular rash? viscidity?
- Veil (if any) - Texture; colour; persistence and location of remains
- Stipe Interior - Colour change(s) on bruising (Cut fruiting body vertically through center).
- In case of Cantharellaceae include in your photograph bisected sporocarp, display cut side up, cut side down, whole sporocarp with ruler and foliage. Include metric scale.
- For the identification of Lactarius also take pictures of milk - colour changes (after exposure wait for half an hour).
- Margin of Cap – Inrolled, Hairy. Induce latex drops to form and Try to photograph showing colour changes.
- Take close up detail of surface texture, especially Lycoperdon and Calvatia. Shape - Split one specimen in half longitudinally to show inside and outside in same frame. If possible, use specimen mature enough to show differentiation of tissues of fertile and sterile areas. (Does not apply to earthstars)
- Earthstars - Take photo from side to show peristome (apical pore) and whether a pedicel is present between the spore case and the basal cup.
- Record - Size, habitat, location, date, whether mature sporocarp has a loose powdery spore mass or a persistent cottony cushion inside; the method of sporocarp opening, and whether sporocarp is hard, soft, or yielding.

- For sclerodermas photography Measure thickness of peridium at the equator, as fresh and as dry.
- For nidulariaceae photography Show cup shape. Show egg colour and number. Show habitat — logs, moss, twigs, etc.

In case of pezizales photography. Show apothecial shape (stipe presence, cup depth). Close up of cup exterior (presence or absence of granules, hairs, or smooth). Cut view showing presence or absence of gel in sterile tissues Peziza. Show disc colour and margin as well as under surface texture. Show and record presence or absence of coloured latex from broken or cut tissues (Does white tissue turn colour when touched to edge?).

Once photographed mushroom specimen are collected from wild, further steps are taken for mushroom identification viz. Identification of genus and species.

To identify the mushroom species collected from different sites, morphological, reproductive, chemical and other characters are taken into consideration. A magnifying glass is used to see the fine morphological characters. Important characters which aid in identification of mushrooms are: colour, size, shape and flesh colour of mushrooms. The colour of the mushrooms can be compared with colour charts. Presence or absence of gills, false gills, pores or teeth, gill arrangement, colour and density must be recorded besides colour, size and shape of the stipe. Presence of rings on the stipe, presence of volva, veil, presence or absence of scales on the cap and stipe should be observed and recorded. Odour of the specimen, taste of the specimens, colour changes, presence of latex should be noted in some species. The cuticle and its degree of detachment, chemical treatment of the specimen and subsequent colour changes are key to identification in some species. A mushroom must be dug a little bit deep along with some substrate so as to get some mycelium. One must try hard to get several developmental stages, viz. button and mature stages of the same mushroom for proper identification. Some samples should be taken to laboratory/home in paper bags for further investigation and their spore prints should be recorded by allowing them to deposit their spores overnight.

How to Obtain Spore Print

Spore prints of most mushrooms can be obtained after returning to the laboratory. However, for very small fruit bodies which may dry out rapidly it is useful to take into the field a set of small containers and papers for making a spore print at the site of collection. Do not refrigerate specimens before making a spore print as they may not produce a print after refrigeration.

1. A spore print is made by placing a mushroom cap (which is mature but not too old) with the stem removed and the spore-bearing gills facing down on to white paper. It can be covered with a box or glass, etc. for protection against air movements and desiccation. A few drops of water placed on a fungus may help to prevent desiccation.

2. After a period of one hour to overnight (depending on the size and condition of the specimen), the spores get deposited on the paper. The spores will adhere to the paper but can be easily brushed off, and therefore require protection in an envelope.

3. The colour of the deposit itself is useful for broad identification purposes, and the spores can be used for later microscopic examination. Spore print colour should be noted soon after they are produced as they may change colour upon drying out, and may also change further after lengthy periods of storage.

4. Label the spore print paper with the code number of the fungal collection. Allow the paper to dry out, then fold it in half with the spores facing inwards. Store spore prints with the corresponding specimen, or in an envelope labelled with the code number. Spore print papers are used after observing gills properly and then selecting contrasting paper colours. Spore prints reveal the colours of spores and to some extent density of gills. Generally spore print resembles the gill colour. Individual spore characters like shape, size and surface features of spores should be recorded by observing them under compound microscope. Spore slides should be prepared in distilled water and, iodine and Melezer's reagent.

Some mushroom groups with their characteristic spore prints are as follows:

- White, Cream and Yellow Spore Print is found in Amanita, Lepiota, Pleurotus, Panus, Lentinellus, Armillariella, Clitocybe
- Pink, Salmon, Redish, Red-Brown spore prints are found in Pluteus, Volvariella, Phyllotopsis
- Rust, Ochre, Chocolate-Brown spore prints are found in Pholiota, Conocybe, Hebelloma, Galerina, Gymnopilus, Agaricus
- Purple-Brown, Purple-Black, Black spore prints are found in Panaeolus, Psilocybe, Coprinus

- Green, Gray-Green, Olive spore prints are found in Chlorophyllum, Phylloporus

PRESERVATION OF MUSHROOMS

Preservation of mushrooms for future use can be done by two methods:

Dry Method: For preserving mushrooms for herbarium purposes, fresh wild mushrooms are either sun dried or dried by means of a heater fan. Gentle heat or hot air is blown over the mushroom specimen in order to save the broad morphological details. When the mushrooms are dry completely they were preserved in air tight zip lock polythene bags. In order to avoid the mycophage insects, small quantity of naphthalene powder is kept in each bag. In case of Morchella species 20-30 mushrooms are tied on a string and hanged in open air under sun. This also avoids growth of moulds.

Wet method: In wet method 70 per cent ethanol is used to preserve mushrooms for shorter periods, viz. one or two months. During prolonged preservation in 70 per cent ethanol, mushrooms release rusty colour which defaces the specimen. For longer duration and in order to retain original sizê and shape of mushrooms they are preserved in 4 per cent formaldehyde which is prepared by mixing methylated sprit (550 ml), 40 per cent formaline (50 ml), glycerol (50 ml) and distilled water (350 ml).

How to start identification from wild habitat Generally macro characters are observed and recorded in field itself because they are fragile and liable to change. Below are 8 things to observe when examining a new mushroom.

1. Habitat – It includes type of trees and topography.
2. Time of year – Mushrooms are generally season specific, but some are strictly confined to one season of the year.
3. Type of Spore bearing surface: Gills /False gills/ Pores/Teeth
4. Stalk present or absent, Stalk colour/shape/ markings
5. Spore print – Spore print colour, spore shape, spore size, spore colour changes with iodine or melezers reagent
6. Bruising when touched - Some mushrooms will turn coloured when scratched
7. Cap description - The colour, markings, and shape of a mushroom cap.
8. Smell/taste – Test a piece of mushroom.

Mushroom Caps

The cap (pileus) of a mushroom helps in mushroom identification by recording following cap parameters:

Size - the cap width and height (at centre) of the smallest and largest mature fruit body in a collection.

Shape – Mushroom caps provide different geometrical shapes to mushrooms. Young and mature fruit bodies should be assessed in side view and top view. At the centre of the pileus there may be a depression *(centrally depressed)*, or a protrusion *(umbonate)*.

Margin - The cap margin should be assessed in terms of side view when cut in half, shape of the edge outline , and surface view of the edge .

Moisture - the cap surface may be dry, or moist. If the cap is gelatinised it may be glutinous (slimy), or viscid (sticky).

Hygrophany – Colour changes from button to mature stages in most of the mushrooms. Colour change in the cap also results from desiccation **Texture** - The cap surface may be smooth or variously uneven. It should be noted whether the texture is due to superficial structures that are easily removed (often derived from the veil), or are part of the cap surface itself. A large range of terms applies to surface texture:

Pits - include the following:

Scrobiculate - shallow pits

Aveolate - deep pits

Lacunose - deep pits surrounded by ridges

Splits - include the following:

Rimose - radially split

Areolate - split into polygonal or irregular shaped blocks

Wrinkles - include the following:

Rivulose – with wavy lines

Rugulose - with undulating wrinkles

Rugose - with coarse wrinkles

Surface powder, hairs, scales - three extreme general categories are:

Glabrous - bald, wax-like surface

Hispid - covered with stiff hairs

Scabrous - surface roughened due to scales

Orientation of particles, fibrils, hairs or scales - may be:

Appressed - scales and fibrils flat on the cap surface

Recurved - base appressed but tips of the scales/ hairs or fibrils turn upwards

Erect - perpendicular to the cap surface

Particles on the surface - include:

Atomate - minute shining particles

Micaceous - glistening minute particles

Pruinose *(pulverulent)* - covered with a fine powder

Furfuraceous (scurfy) - bran-sized scales like dandruff

Granulose - powder composed of particles as big as grains of salt

Fibrils lying on the surface - include the following:

Fibrillose - hyphae forming visible fibrils on the surface

Downy or canescent - soft downy surface

Floccose - coarser, loosely cotton-like surface

Tomentose - densely matted and woolly surface

Matted fibrillose - fibrils matted or interwoven

Fibrils/hairs perpendicular to the surface - include the following:

Pubescent - very short, soft hairs

Veutinous - short, fine, velvety flexible hairs

Villose - long fine hairs

Hirsute - abundant, stiff, inflexible hairs

Fibrils combining to form scales - include the following:

Squamose - scaly surface, large scales

Squamulose - small scales

Squarrose - erect scales

Punctate - dotted with minute scales

Scabrous - surface roughened

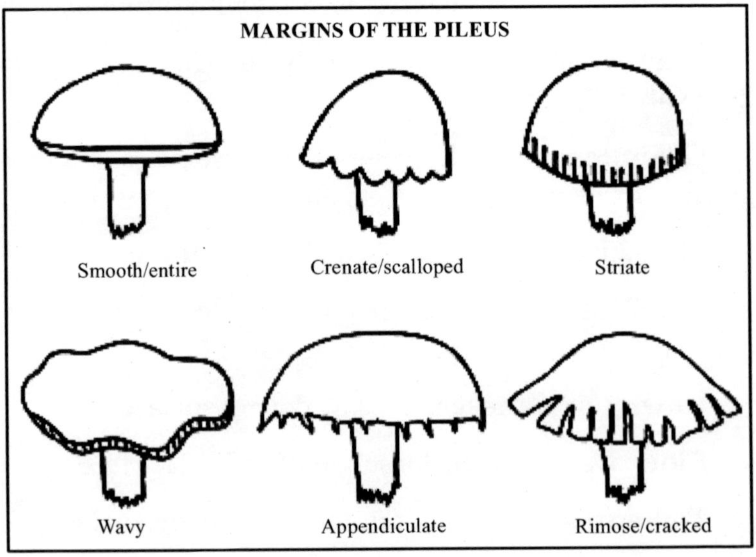

Simple way of mushroom identification is to look whether a Mushroom has :Gills, Pores, or Teeth

One of the more useful traits to examine when trying to identify mushrooms is their method of spore dispersal. This is simply the means by which the mushroom produces and distributes its spores. You can think of spores as mushroom seeds. Mushrooms produce and drop millions of spores with the intention that some of them will germinate, fuse together and grow into new mycelium. Mycelium is the actual organism from which mushrooms are created. To make a comparison: the mycelium is the tree, the mushrooms it produces are the apples and the spores created by the mushrooms are the apple seeds. The tissue that creates these spores (called the hymenium) is found on few different types of structures like gills, pores and teeth. Some Mushrooms disperse spores without using gills, pores or teeth.

THE GILLED MUSHROOMS

Mushroom gills are the thin, papery structures that hang vertically under the cap. The sole purpose of these gills, called lamellae, is to produce spores. The spores are then dropped from the gills by the millions where they are scattered by wind currents to reach their specific habitat for germination and start new generation. Examining the gills is important when identifying mushrooms.

SPECIES WITH PORES

Another structures used for spore dispersal instead of a gill is known as a pore. Mushroom pores appear as small holes on the underside of the cap. This pore surface appears sponge-like. These holes are actually the ends of a series of tubes within the mushrooms cap. Spores are produced on the sides of these tubes and eventually they are released where they fall down the tube. Once out of the pore, and into the air, wind, animals and insects will further carry them from there. When trying to identify mushrooms, be sure to note the pore surface. Traits such as colour, pore size, and pore pattern may help indicate the species. Two common groups of mushrooms with pores are boletes (the Boletus genus) and polypores. Some key characteristics of each are:

Most boletes have a stalk, an umbrella-shaped top, and disperse spores through the small pores underneath the cap. This pore-laden area beneath the cap is often quite spongy. Unlike boletes, polypores almost always grow on wood and never on the ground. They're found on rotting trees, stumps and logs. Polypores are normally shaped like shelves, hence the term "bracket fungi". They don't have caps or a district stipe.

Tooth mushrooms: Another method of spore dispersal is through teeth (also called apines). Tooth fungi have long thin "teeth" that hang downward and produce spores. They have basically the same setup and function as gilled fungi: only the process is done through their spiny teeth. Although there are fewer mushrooms with teeth than their gilled and pored counterparts.

Mushroom Gills/Pores

The following observations are used to describe the shape, orientation, arrangement, spacing and attachment of gills/ pores

Attachment to stipe - described as follows:

Decurrent - extending down the stem

Adnate - broadly attached

Adnexed - partially attached

Free - not attached

Sinuate - notched near the attachment

Receding - attached at first becoming free later.

Spacing - cut off the stem and observe the radial pattern of the gills to see if they are crowded, well

Spaced apart *(distant),* or arbitrarily somewhat in between *(close or subdistant).*

LAMELLAE/GILL SPACING

Distant Close Crowded

Thickness - in side view, the gills may be *thin, broad* or *ventricose* (swollen in middle).

Margin - the edge of the gills may be smooth or variously uneven as seen through a hand lens, e.g.

Crenate, serrate or eroded : The edge may differ in colour to the face, and may be *glistening* or *nmbriate* (minutely fringed, often due to presence of cystidia - then referred to as *cystidiate).*

Branching and anastomoses - the gills may be unbranched, dichotomously branched *(bifurcate)* or may be joined by anastomosing interconnections *(costate).*

Length, Sometimes the gills may not run all the way from the stem to the cap. These are called short gills and may be helpful in making a proper identification.

Lamellulae - short gills which extend only part of the way from the cap margin to the stipe.

Lamellules may be *absent* or *abundant* and of two or more sizes.

Tiers - the number of distinct lengths of lamellulae.

Number - the number of gills per cap varies between fungi and is largely related to the spacing. A standard way of recording this data is to count the number of gills (L) and lamellules (I) per half a cap, resulting in a notation for each collection (such as L = 10-14, I = 22-28).

SOME UNIQUE EXAMPLES

Here are some mushrooms that don't reproduce through gills, pores or teeth:

Chanterelles: The edibe chanterelle has structures that appear forked but these are actually "false gills". Unlike true gills, they are not separates features that can be individually picked off. Instead they appear as melted folds on the underside of a mushroom. Learn to distinguish true from false gills if attempting to pick chanterelles. Chanterelles drop spores from the undersides of their curled caps, which are often smooth.

Stinkhorn: These mushrooms produce spores in a foul smelling jelly that covers the top of the mushroom. Flies are attracted and spread the spores after landing.

Puffballs, release their spores through a hole in the top (ostiole) or when the mushroom ruptures.

Coral mushrooms: The hymenium (spore creating tissue) of most coral fungi occurs as a microscopic layer covering all the branches. Spores simply drop from there.

Cup mushrooms have a spore-bearing surface on the inside of the cup with no pores or gills.

Morel: Morel mushroom contains spore-producing sacs along the insides of its pits or wrinkles.

Mushroom Stipe

Stipe: This structure helps in spore dispersal by keeping cap up in the air. Certain polypores, puffballs, and earthstars do not have stipe. The majority of gilled mushrooms do have one, commonly found at the center of the cap. The stalk is an important feature to examine when identifying wild mushrooms. The shape and tissue composition of stipes is described by the following parameters

Size - diameter at the base, middle and apex of the smallest and largest fruit body in a collection (mm). Is it long, thing, or fatter on the bottom?

Shape - in cross-section, e.g. if circular *(terete)* or *compressed.* The stipe shape in longitudinal view can be extremely variable, e.g. *cylindrical. clavate, tapering.* The base of the stipe must also be taken into consideration, e.g. *bulbous, radicating*.

Attachment - whether the stem has central or lateral attachment to the cap.

Texture - similar terms as used for pileus are applied to stipes. The distribution of any surface features along the stipe should be noted. A few extra terms include:

Reticulate - interlocking pattern of ridges or wrinkles.

Glandular - coloured dots or small scales especially near the stipe apex.

Other options - longitudinally striate, ridged, veined etc.

Interior - *solid, stuffed, chambered* (Iacunose), or *hollow.*

Consistency – fragile, robust, cartilaginous, fibrous, woody, corky, chalky etc. Some fungi have a tough outer layer.

The Universal Veil

As the mushroom expands the universal veil ruptures. In mature fruit bodies it may be absent or remain as scales on the pileus surface and/or as a volva. The lower stipe may also have multiple zones of universal veil tissue.

Scales - patches of veil remnants on the cap surface. The texture of scales can be:

- Powdery
- Appressed
- Pyramidal warts

Volva - a cup-shaped structure at the base of the stipe formed from the universal veil. The volva may occur as a separate tissue (loose sack) or may be attached to a bulbous base indicated only by the presence of a rim. Terms used to describe the volva include:

Membranous - thin free from base

Attached - inconspicuous tissue on base

Saccate - like a loose bag

Powdery, friable, ragged bands.

The Partial Veil

In young fruit bodies the partial veil extends from the cap margin to the stipe and covers the gills during development, later breaking to expose the mature gills. A partial veil is absent in many mushroom. Both partial and universal veil remnants may form multiple bands on the stem. Texture of the intact partial veil varies between the following forms:

Membranous - a thin uniform sheath.

Cortina - a cobweb-like structure. Cortinoid-type veils either soon disappear (i.e. they are *evanescent),* or remain as an indistinct *ffbrillose zone* on the stipe.

Annulus (ring) - a persistent veil present on the stipe of mature fruit bodies.

Appendiculate cap margin - a rim on the cap margin formed from the partial veil.

Annulus position - rings may occur in the following locations:

Superior position - near the stipe apex.

Central

Basal (inferior).

Some mushrooms have uniqe stipe:

- Bracket fungus - no stalk
- Morels (Morchella species) - hollow
- Shaggy mane (*Coprinus comatus*) - hollow, cylindrical, bulbous at base
- *Hypholoma capnoides* - enlarged at base, covered in hairs
- Shiitake (*Lentinula edodes*) - stem bruises brown

SHAPES OF THE SRIPE

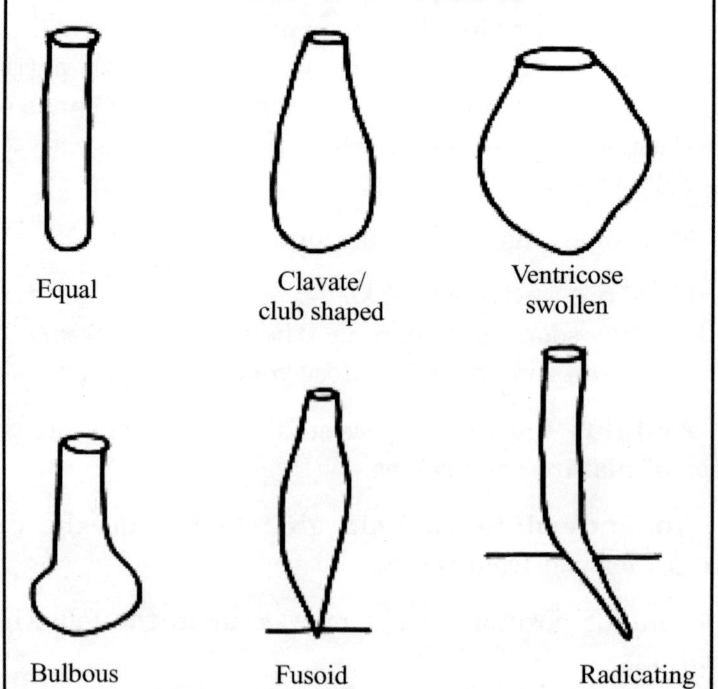

Mushroom Colours

Mushrooms have a rainbow of colours, thus a variety of terminology is used to describe these colours as described

Aeruginose (malachite-green), the colour of oxidized copper)

Alutaceous (light leather coloured, usually interpreted as light tan or medium yellow brown)

Argillaceous (clay colour, resembling ochraceous-cinnamon-brown)

Avellaneous (pale pinkish gray);

Azure (Sky Blue in colour)

Aadious (Dark red brown)

Bay (Red-brown approaching but lighter than chestnut)

Beige (Light grayish yellowish brown)

Benzo brown (Pale purplish brown, dark brownish, violaceous fuscous, gray brown with a pinkish tinge)

Binomial (blackish brown, a warm dark brown colour, like sepia, dark yellow-brown)

Bister (blackish brown, a warm dark brown colour, like sepia, dark yellow-brown)

Bone brown (Dark vinacious brown)

Buckhorn brown (Dull yellowish brown)

Buff (A pale yellow toned with gray-brown, i.e., a dingy yellowish brown or very pale tan)

Burnt sienna (Watery strong red-brown, dark orange brown)

Chestnut — dark red-brown

Chrome-yellow — intense or strong yellow; also can be deep orange or even reddish orange

Cigar — brown a dark blackish brown, like that of the tobacco found in a cigar

Ciliate — having a fringe of hair-like ciliae appearing fringed

Cinereous — ash-coloured, dirty white

Cinnabar — deep bright rather orange red

Cinnamon — a light brown with a little pink

Cinnamon-buff — pale dingy tan

Cinnamon-drab — violaceous brown with only a faint cinnamon tint, pinkish gray brown

Crimson — rich deep red inclining to purple

Ferruginous (rusty)

Fulvous (rusty brown or tawny)

Fuscous (grayish or grayish brown)

Glaucous (greenish)

Incarnate (flesh coloured)

Isabella (yellowish brown to light olive brown)

Isabelline (yellowish brown to light olive brown)

Livid (grayish or bluish gray)

Lurid (usually "dark red";)

Lutescent (staining yellow)

Ochre (brownish yellow)

Ochraceous (brownish yellowish)

Olivaceous (olive—the greenish colour)

Rubescent (blushing reddish or pinkish)

Sordid (dingy)

Vinaceous (purplish red)

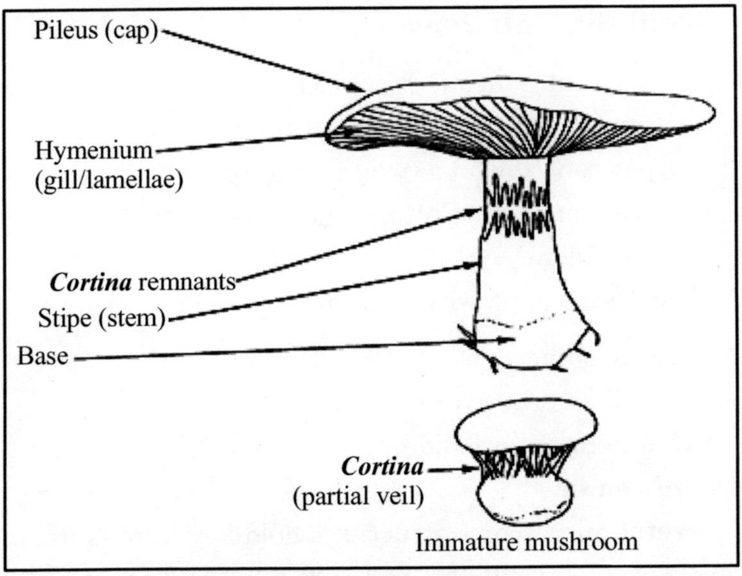

Basic Morphology of Mushrooms

Equipment and reagents required for mushroom microscopy

Mushroom microscopy is an excellent insight into the mushroom world, because it reveals a number of structures which are sufficient for delimiting even closely resembling mushrooms. For observing microscopic characters a compound microscope with 100 X oil immersion objective is best suited. Micrometer microscope with an attached camera Lucida is good for observing and drawing microscopic structures of mushrooms. Sharp, razor blades for disection. Sharp razor, fine forceps, dissecting needles, are of prime importance. Sharp drawing pencil for drawing the observed structures. Standardized data sheets Glass microscope slides and cover slips are other much needed articles.

Mounting solutions:

- 3 per cent aqueous (w/v) KOH
- 10 per cent aqueous (v/v) Ammonia
- 1 per cent aqueous (w/v) Congo red
- 1 per cent *(w/v)* Cotton blue in lactic acid
- water alone

Melzer's reagent with chloral hydrate:

- 1.5 g iodine
- 100 g chloral hydrate
- 5 g potassium iodide
- 100 mL water

Several microscopic structures hold key in mushroom identification but following three characters are often resorted to.

1. Spores are often the most important feature.

2. The hymenium (fertile layer - basidia and cystidia) and the pileipellis or peridium (cap cuticle) are also important.

3. Hymenial trama, stipitopellis, caulocystidia, veil remnants, and the pileus and stipe trama.

Basic mushroom microscopic structures

Spores- Note the colour, size, shape, wall ornamentation and thickness, amyloid or dextrinoid staining with Melzer's reagent.

Basidia - Impotant to observe is colour, size, shape, and number of sterigma (spore-bearing projections).

Trama - composed of hyphae which form patterns and layers in the gills, cap and stem.

Cystidia - swollen hyphal tips. Note their colour, size, shape and abundance. These include:

Pleurocystidia - on the gill faces

Cheilocystidia - on the gill edges

Pileocystidia - on the cap stem

Caulocystidia - on the stem

Cuticle of a fungal organ

Pileipellis - skin on cap (pileus)

Stipitipellis - skin on stem (stipe)

Veil remnants - composed of hyphae which can have a characteristic colour, size, shape, or arrangement.

Clamp connections - often occur on fungal hyphae. Note their presence, or absence, abundance and distribution in different tissues.

How to Proceed for mushroom Microscopy

Squashing Tissue

The easy way to observe microscopic world of mushrooms is to place a small piece of mushroom tissue on a slide, cover it with a cover slip and gently tap the cover slip until the tissue is squashed flat. This technique causes the tissue to flatten outward and separates the individual structures, allowing easy microscopic observation. For observing natural colour patterns fresh mushroom piece may be mounted on microscope slides in a small drop of water. Dried specimens may be revived by mounting material in 3 per cent or 5 per cent KOH or 10 per cent ammonia. An aqueous solution of Congo red stains hyphal walls, but it is usually best to observe the colour of walls in water, KOH or ammonia first.

Sectioning Tissue

Hand sectioning with a blade can reveal structures such as the cuticle and gills. Air-dried mushroom may need to be rehydrated by soaking in 95 per cent ethanol or KOH for a few minutes then quickly dipped in water before sectioning in this manner. Adding 10 per cent glycerol can make sections or slides to remain intact for longer periods. Cut the fruiting body in half longitudinally. Use the tangential plane to make thin sections of the gills for examination under the microscope -one at the gill face, one at the gill edge, and one at the gill trama. The pileipellis may also be examined in tangential plane, but it is usually preferable to examine it in radial plane. The stages described above should result in 6 main slide preparations of thin tissue slices, that can be examined under the microscope:

- radial section of the cap cuticle (pileipellis).
- radial section of cap flesh (trama).
- tangential section of the gills (face and edge) and trama of the gills and cap.
- radial section of the stem cuticle (stipitopellis).
- radial section of stem flesh (trama),
- spores obtained from the spore print.

Observing and Measuring Microscopic Structures

Measurements can be made by using a special eyepiece with a scale called an ocular micrometer or eyepiece micrometer. Calibration must be done before measurements. Include a range of specimens for measurements and other attributes such as Shapes and ornamentations

Colours and chemical reactions - For all microscopic characters in water, KOH and Melzer's reagent, record the following.

- Some tissues (particularly spores) may react to Melzer's reagent by becoming blue (amyloid reaction) or brown (dextrinoid reaction). The reaction may be enhanced by gentle warming.
- In 1 per cent cotton blue in lactic acid, the wall of spores or other structures may stain dark blue. This is called apositive cyanophilic reaction.
- Many fungi have distinct pigmentation and it is important to observe the location of these pigments. For example, pigmentation may occur inside cells (intracellular), between the cells (intercellular), or on cell walls (encrusting).

Spore Characters of Mushrooms

Spore acts as a propagule or seed of a mushroom. Mushrooms bear a variety of spore colours. shapes. sizes and walls. Thus mushroom spore characters act as fingerprint in delimiting genera and species.

Mounting spores: A spore print is best source of spores. Mature spores for describing should be obtained from spore prints by scraping a small amount off the print with a blade or forceps or a painting brush . These spores are then mounted in water or 3 per cent KOH or 10 per cent ammonia.

Spore colour- the colour of the spores in water and in KOH or ammonia is usually recorded under microscope. How Melzer's reagent stains a spore is observed to determine if the spores are amyloid (blue reaction) or dextrnoid (red/brown reaction).

Measuring spores - A minimum of 20 to 25 spores per specimen is measured. A list of shortest and longest spores is recorded the narrowest and the broadest spores are recorded. Their average length. Average breadth, average ratio of length to breadth is also written. The dimensions of spores must be measured in face and side (profile) view. Note that spores roating in a mounting medium will have random orientations and only those seen completely in face or profile view should be measured. Record the medium in which measurements are made as this can effect spore sizes. It is usual to include the apiculus but not any ornamentation or perisporium in spore size measurements, but it is important to record what structures were measured.

Spore symmetry- Mushrooms spores are commonly bilaterally asymmetrical (inequilateral). Gasteromycetes and truffle-like fungi usually have spores that are bilaterally symmetrical (equilateral).

Spore shape - Mushroom spores have a diverse shapes which can be described by many descriptive terms. Shapes that are in between these broad categories may be described by applying the prefix 'sub', e.g. subglobose is not quite globose but close to it. The shape and size of the hilar appendix (point of attachment to the basidium before separation) should be recorded, e .g. rounded, beaked, broken or entire. Also the spore apex (opposite end to the hilar appendix) may be rounded or attenuated (mucronate or rostrate).

Main Spore Shapes:

Ellipsoid - sides are curved and ends rounded

Ovoid - egg-shaped, one end larger than the other

Globose - spherical

Oblong/cylindrical - ends round, sides parallel

Fusiform - tapering of both ends

Citriniform - lemon-shaped, ends of the spores with a beak-like projection

Amygdaliform - almond-shaped

Phaseoliform - bean-shaped

Angular - various angular spore shapes

Spore Wall Structure and Ornamentation

The spore wall is an important diagnostic character. Details of spore walls and ornamentation must be observed under the high power microscope objective (100x). In some cases, high power light microscopy will reveal fine ornamentation of spores which appear smooth at lower magnifications. For all spores regardless of whether they are smooth or ornamented, the spore wall thickness and the number of distinct layers should be noted. At the apex of the spore, the wall may be conspicuously thin and modified into a beak like structure.

Six main types of spore ornamentation:

Verrucose - warts

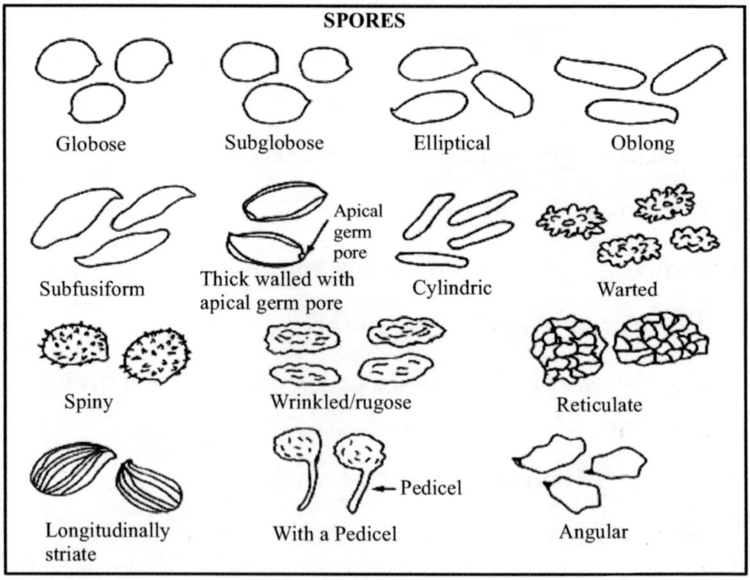

Nodulose - large knobbly ornaments

Ridged - ranging from striate to ribbed with large ridges

Punctate - small projections

Echinate - long sharp pointed spines

Reticulate- ornaments with interconnections in a regular or irregular pattern

Mycelial Chracters

Observe under 400x-1000x magnification:

Mycelium characteristics generally fall into one of the following categories for each form and colour

FORM:

Linear

Rhizomorphic

Cottony

Zonate

Matted or appressed

Powdered

Unique formations

COLOUR:

White

Yellow/orange/pink

Brown

Blue

Black

Multicoloured

Identifying Mushrooms through Bruising and Bleeding

Certain mushrooms will change colours when damaged or injured. Cutting into a mushroom and observing any colour changes can be very important when trying to determine what it is.

Mushroom Bruising: While identifying mushrooms, check for bruising by nicking mushroom and watching for any colour change. Try this within 30 minutes of picking.

Mushroom Bleeding: Certain mushrooms will exude a red milky liquid latex substance when they are cut. The exact reason for the latex is not fully understood. It is believed to be a method of defense, due to its bitter taste and the fact that it dries to form a protective coating around the injury. This keeps out bacteria and other contaminants. Some of the most famous bleeding mushrooms are those in the Lactarius genus. These are called the milky caps due to the milky latex they exude upon injury. If you're observing any bleeding during mushroom identification, be sure to note both the initial liquid colour and the final dried colour.

Best examples are *Agaricus bisporus* (white button mushroom) - Usually bruises pinkish.

Boletus campestris - Bruises blue or blue-green. Many yellow-pored boletes bruise blue.

Psilocybe cubensis - The stems bruise blue or blue-green.

Russula rubescens - Bruises reddish, and then slowly turns to black.

Mycena haematopus - Bleeds purplish.

Lactarius helvus (maple syrup milky cap) - Bleeds colourless latex that smells like maple syrup.

Lactarius chrysorrheus - Bleeds white latex that dries to a deeper yellow.

USE OF SENSES IN MUSHROOM IDENTIFICATION

Test for smell by crushing a piece of the cap and examining the odor. Mushrooms may or may not smell. Some well-known mushroom scents:

Chanterelles (Cantharellus species) - fruity like apricots

Many Agaricus species - almonds

Marasmius scorodonius - garlic

Stinkhorns - An unpleasant "rotting" smell.

Taste test: Take a small piece of the cap and place it in your mouth on the tongue for a few seconds. Then spit it out, do not swallow! Always wash mouth after tasting a mushroom.

Use of Chemicals in Mushroom Identification

Mushroom surfaces, flesh, and spores react to the application of certain chemicals. Three chemicals are used by mycologists to identify mushrooms.

Ammonia (NH4OH, Ammonium Hydroxide): Ammonia is mainly used for boletes identification. Place a drop of ammonia on a fresh bolete's cap, stem, sliced flesh, and pore surface. Note any colour change.

KOH (Potassium Hydroxide): KOH (aqueous 3-5 per cent) is used in the identification of many mushrooms, including boletes, polypores, and gilled mushrooms. Apply a drop of KOH on the cap, or on flesh, stipe, sliced flesh, and pore surface. Note any colour changes that take place. It colours yellow Agaricus and Amanita; changes magenta or olive Russula and Lactarius. Deep red or black reactions many be found in gilled mushrooms. Black are important in delimting polypores. Also note if a mushroom does not react with KOH.

Iron Salts ($FeSO_4$ 10 per cent): $FeSO_4$ tests boletes and russulas. For boletes, place a drop on the cap, stem, sliced flesh, and pore surface; for russulas, place a drop on the stem surface.

KEY TO MAJOR GROUPS OF MUSHROOMS

1.	Mushroom growing on other mushrooms or the decayed remains of other mushrooms.	Mycotrophs
1.	Mushroom not growing on other mushrooms.	2
2.	Mushroom with gills on its underside.	3
2.	Gills absent.	5
3.	Growing shelflike on wood (or, if not, then gills concentric rather than radial); mushroom very tough and leathery, corky, or woody (try tearing it in	Polypores

	half); gills tough and hard, sometimes maze-like; cap frequently (but not always) with concentric zones of color.	
3.	Not completely as above.	4
4.	Gills running down the stem, not platelike and thus not easily separable from the cap and stem (try removing an entire "gill" with your fingers or a sharp object); mushroom usually not growing on wood.	Chanterelles and Trumpets
4.	Gills not as above; mushroom growing on wood or elsewhere.	Gilled Mushrooms
5.	Mushroom with pores on its underside (they may be very tiny; use a hand lens if unsure).	6
5.	Pores absent.	9
6.	Stem absent—or, if present, lateral.	Polypores
6.	Stem present and central.	7
7.	Flesh in stem tough.	Polypores
7.	Flesh in stem soft.	8

8.	Cap round in outline; pore surface not running down the stem, or only slightly running down the stem; spore print not white.	Boletes
8.	Cap round to irregular in outline; pore surface running down the stem; spore print white.	Polypores
9.	Mushroom with spines or "teeth"—either on the underside of a cap, or hanging from a branched structure, or clumped together in an indistinct mass.	Toothed Mushrooms
9.	Spines or teeth absent.	10
10.	Mushroom covered in some part with a foul-smelling slime; arising from a soft underground "egg"; variously shaped (like a club or stick, like crab claws, like a lantern, like a Wiffle ball, etc.); frequently found in urban settings, but also found in woods.	Stinkhorns
10.	Not as above.	11
11.	Mushroom shaped like a cup, a saucer, a goblet, a standing rabbit ear, a bowl, (etc.), with or without a stem.	12

11.	Mushroom not shaped as above.	13
12.	Goblet or cup with tiny "eggs" inside; mushroom very small.	Bird's Nest Fungi
12.	Eggs absent; mushroom variously sized.	Cup Fungi
13.	Mushroom more or less shaped like a ball, or like a ball raised up on a stem, or like a ball set on a starfish.	Puffballs
13.	Not as above.	14
14.	Mushroom with a clearly defined, more or less central stem that is separate from a clearly defined cap.	15
14.	Mushroom without a clearly defined cap and stem.	19
15.	Cap shape convex to centrally depressed or vase-shaped; under surface smooth, wrinkled, or gill-like; rarely fruiting in spring except in warm coastal areas.	Chanterelles and Trumpets
15.	Cap shape oval, pointed, lobed, saddle-shaped, irregular, or thimble-like (never vase-shaped or convex); undersurface absent, or hard to see or	16

	convex); undersurface absent, or hard to see or define; many (but definitely not all) species fruiting in spring.	
16.	Stem completely hollow, or hollow with cottony fibers inside; cap with pits and ridges, or longitudinally wrinkled, or fairly smooth (never lobed or convoluted); without reddish or reddish brown shades; found in spring.	True Morels and Verpas
16.	Not completely as above.	17
17.	Most (but not all) species found in spring (in north-temperature regions); cap lobed, convoluted, "brainlike," or irregular, with brownish or reddish brown to reddish shades (never black, white, or gray when fresh).	False Morels
17.	Not completely as above.	18
18.	Found in summer and fall (or spring in warm coastal areas); cap lobed, saddle-shaped, or irregular and whitish, grayish, brownish, or black; stem surface ribbed or "pocketed" in some species.	Saddles

18.	Not completely as above.	Oddballs and Misfits
19.	Mushroom thin-fleshed and vase-shaped or tubular-or vase-shaped and fleshy, with scales on the cap surface or with several caps arising from a shared stem.	Chanterelles and Trumpets
19.	Not as above.	Jelly Fungi and Others
20.	Mushroom jelly-like or semi-gelatinous; formless, brain-like, glob-like, or lobed; usually growing on wood or on plants or other mushrooms.	Jelly Fungi and Others
20.	Not completely as above.	21
21.	Mushroom shaped like a branched or unbranched club or stick--or shaped like a coral (or a head of cauliflower); most species growing on the ground but a few growing on wood.	Clubs and Corals
21.	Not completely as above.	22
22.	Mushroom growing on wood; shaped more or less like a fan or a kidney; underside smooth or vaguely wrinkled, but without pores or gills-or,	Crust Fungi

	mushroom without a clearly defined cap or stem, appearing more or less like a crust or a spreading surface that lacks a mushroom; usually growing on the undersides of downed logs.	
22.	Not completely as above.	Oddballs and Misfits

Final identification up to species level can be done by comparing the recorded characters of mushrooms with standard field guides and keys of experts. Field guide of David and Pegler and Brain Spooner's guide to mushrooms, Larengent's (1973) and Simon and Schuster's Guide to mushrooms (1998) are best for the identification of mushrooms. Online resources like "Mushworld.com" and "mycoweb" "Michel Kuo- Mushroom Expert.com" can help to identify mushrooms up to species level.